# The Gratitude Effect: Harnessing the Power of Thankfulness for Success

Memphis Andy

# Copyright © [2023]

## Title: The Gratitude Effect: Harnessing the Power of Thankfulness for Success
## Author's: Memphis Andy



This book was printed and published by [Publisher's: **Memphis Andy**] in [2023]

**ISBN:**

# TABLE OF CONTENT

## Chapter 1: The Power of Gratitude    07

Understanding Gratitude

The Science behind Gratitude

Cultivating a Grateful Mindset

## Chapter 2: The Benefits of Gratitude    13

Improved Mental Health

Increased Happiness

Enhanced Relationships

Physical Health Benefits

## Chapter 3: Gratitude for Personal Growth    21

Developing Self-Awareness through Gratitude

Overcoming Challenges with Gratitude

Setting and Achieving Goals with Gratitude

# Chapter 7: Practicing Gratitude Daily



Creating a Gratitude Journal

Expressing Gratitude to Others

Incorporating Gratitude Rituals into Your Life

# Chapter 8: Overcoming Obstacles to Gratitude



Dealing with Negativity and Resentment

Cultivating Gratitude during Difficult Times

Overcoming Gratitude Blocks

# Chapter 9: Spreading the Gratitude Effect



Teaching Gratitude to Children

Sharing Gratitude in Your Community

Creating a Ripple Effect of Gratitude

# Chapter 10: The Gratitude Journey Continues 63

Reinforcing Gratitude Habits

Embracing a Lifetime of Thankfulness

Gratitude as a Transformational Tool for Success

# Chapter 1: The Power of Gratitude

## Understanding Gratitude

Gratitude is a powerful emotion that has the ability to transform our lives and bring about positive change. In this subchapter, we will delve into the concept of gratitude and explore its importance in our daily lives. Whether you are a student, a professional, a parent, or simply someone seeking personal growth, understanding gratitude is essential for achieving success and fulfillment.

Gratitude, at its core, is a mindset of appreciation and thankfulness for the blessings and experiences we have in life. It goes beyond merely saying "thank you" and extends to a deep sense of recognition and value for the people, things, and opportunities that come our way. When we practice gratitude, we acknowledge the goodness in our lives and embrace the positive energy it brings.

One of the key reasons why gratitude is so important is its ability to shift our focus from what we lack to what we have. In today's fast-paced and competitive world, it is easy to get caught up in the cycle of always wanting more. However, gratitude helps us cultivate a sense of contentment and appreciation for what we already possess. This shift in perspective not only brings us joy and happiness but also allows us to attract more abundance into our lives.

Moreover, gratitude has a profound impact on our mental and physical well-being. Numerous studies have shown that practicing gratitude regularly can reduce stress, anxiety, and depression. It boosts our immune system, improves sleep quality, and enhances overall mental resilience. By consciously practicing gratitude, we can create a more positive and fulfilling life.

Additionally, gratitude strengthens our relationships and fosters a sense of connection with others. When we express our gratitude towards someone, it not only makes them feel valued and appreciated but also strengthens the bond between us. Gratitude acts as a powerful tool for building and nurturing meaningful connections, whether it is with our loved ones, colleagues, or even strangers.

In conclusion, understanding gratitude is crucial for everyone, regardless of their background or goals in life. By embracing gratitude, we can shift our perspective, improve our well-being, and cultivate stronger relationships. The power of gratitude lies in its ability to transform our lives and unlock our true potential. So, let us embark on the journey of gratitude and harness its incredible power for our success and happiness.

**The Science behind Gratitude**

In this subchapter, we will dive deep into the scientific aspects of gratitude and explore how it impacts our lives. Gratitude is not just a vague concept or a mere expression of appreciation; it has a profound effect on our mental, emotional, and physical well-being. Understanding the science behind gratitude can help us harness its power and incorporate it into our lives for greater success and happiness.

Research conducted over the years has consistently shown that practicing gratitude can lead to numerous benefits. Studies have found that individuals who regularly express gratitude experience lower levels of stress and depression. Grateful people also report higher levels of life satisfaction, happiness, and overall well-being. But what exactly happens in our brains and bodies that contribute to these positive outcomes?

Neuroscience has played a crucial role in unraveling the mysteries of gratitude. It has been discovered that when we feel and express gratitude, our brain releases a surge of dopamine and serotonin, often referred to as the "feel-good" chemicals. These neurotransmitters are responsible for regulating our mood and emotions, giving us a sense of pleasure and contentment. As a result, gratitude rewires our brain, making us more resilient to negative thoughts and emotions.

Moreover, gratitude has a profound impact on our relationships. Research has shown that expressing gratitude towards others strengthens social bonds and fosters a sense of connection. When we show appreciation for someone's actions or kindness, it not only makes them feel valued but also deepens our own sense of empathy and compassion. This positive feedback loop enhances our interpersonal relationships, paving the way for more meaningful connections and a supportive social network.

Furthermore, gratitude has been found to improve physical health. Studies have revealed that grateful individuals have lower blood pressure, better sleep quality, and stronger immune systems. It is believed that the reduction in stress and the overall positive mindset associated with gratitude contribute to these physical benefits.

Understanding the science behind gratitude underscores its importance in our lives. By cultivating gratitude, we can reap the rewards of improved mental health, enhanced relationships, and better physical well-being. Whether through keeping a gratitude journal, expressing appreciation to others, or simply taking a moment to reflect on our blessings, incorporating gratitude into our daily lives is a powerful tool for success and happiness.

## Cultivating a Grateful Mindset

In today's fast-paced and competitive world, it is easy to get caught up in the hustle and bustle of everyday life and forget to appreciate the little things. However, cultivating a grateful mindset is crucial for our overall well-being and success. In this subchapter, we will explore the importance of being grateful and how it can positively impact various aspects of our lives.

Gratitude is a powerful tool that has been proven to enhance our mental, emotional, and physical health. When we practice gratitude, we shift our focus from what is lacking in our lives to what we already have. This simple shift in perspective can lead to a more positive outlook and increased happiness. Numerous studies have shown that individuals who regularly express gratitude experience lower levels of stress and depression, improved sleep quality, and increased resilience in the face of challenges.

Being grateful also strengthens our relationships with others. When we express gratitude towards others, it not only makes them feel appreciated but also fosters a sense of connection and goodwill. Gratitude has the power to mend broken relationships, enhance communication, and create a supportive and harmonious environment. By cultivating a grateful mindset, we can attract more positive and meaningful relationships into our lives.

Furthermore, gratitude plays a significant role in our professional lives. When we approach our work with a grateful mindset, we become more engaged, motivated, and productive. Gratitude helps us recognize the efforts of our colleagues and fosters a sense of teamwork and collaboration. It also enables us to find joy and fulfillment in our work, leading to increased job satisfaction and success.

Practicing gratitude is not limited to specific moments or situations. It is a mindset that can be cultivated throughout our daily lives. By incorporating simple practices such as keeping a gratitude journal, expressing appreciation to others, or taking a moment to reflect on the blessings in our lives, we can gradually develop a grateful mindset.

In conclusion, cultivating a grateful mindset is essential for our overall well-being and success. By embracing gratitude, we can experience improved mental and emotional health, enhanced relationships, and increased professional fulfillment. So, let us make a conscious effort to embrace gratitude in our lives and harness its transformative power for a happier and more successful future.

# Chapter 2: The Benefits of Gratitude

## Improved Mental Health

In our fast-paced and demanding world, it is easy to get caught up in the hustle and bustle of everyday life. We often find ourselves overwhelmed, stressed, and anxious, forgetting to take a moment to appreciate the little things that make life worth living. This is where the importance of being grateful comes into play.

Gratitude is a powerful tool that can transform our lives and improve our mental health. It is the act of acknowledging and appreciating the good things in our lives, big or small, and cultivating a sense of thankfulness for what we have. When we practice gratitude regularly, we shift our focus from negativity to positivity, from lack to abundance, and from stress to serenity.

Research has shown that gratitude has a profound impact on our mental well-being. Studies have found that grateful individuals experience lower levels of depression and anxiety. By focusing on the positive aspects of our lives, we are able to reduce the power of negative emotions and reframe our mindset. Gratitude activates the brain's reward system, releasing feel-good chemicals such as dopamine and serotonin, which promote a sense of happiness and contentment.

Furthermore, being grateful helps us build resilience and cope with adversity. When faced with challenges, having a grateful mindset allows us to find silver linings, learn from difficult experiences, and grow stronger. It helps us shift our perspective and see setbacks as opportunities for growth rather than as failures. This resilience not only improves our mental health but also empowers us to navigate life's ups and downs with a greater sense of ease and grace.

Practicing gratitude is not limited to specific circumstances or accomplishments. It is a mindset that can be cultivated every day. Whether it is writing a gratitude journal, expressing appreciation to loved ones, or simply taking a moment to reflect on what we are grateful for, incorporating gratitude into our lives can have a profound impact on our mental well-being.

So, the next time you find yourself caught in the chaos of life, take a step back and remind yourself of the importance of being grateful. Embrace the power of thankfulness and watch as it transforms your mental health, allowing you to live a more fulfilling and joyful life.

Remember, gratitude is not just a one-time practice; it is a lifelong journey that can shape and enhance every aspect of our lives, leading to true success and happiness. Start today, and let the gratitude effect change your life for the better.

## Increased Happiness

Happiness is a universal pursuit that transcends age, gender, and cultural boundaries. It is a state of mind that everyone strives to achieve, yet often feels elusive in the fast-paced and demanding world we live in. However, what if I told you that the key to unlocking this ever-elusive happiness lies within a simple yet powerful concept - gratitude? In this subchapter, we will explore the profound impact that increased gratitude can have on our overall well-being and happiness.

The importance of being grateful cannot be overstated. When we practice gratitude, we shift our focus from what is lacking in our lives to what we already have. It is a mindset that allows us to appreciate the present moment, acknowledging the blessings and opportunities that surround us. By cultivating gratitude, we develop a greater sense of contentment and fulfillment, leading to increased happiness.

Research has shown that individuals who regularly practice gratitude experience a wide range of benefits. Firstly, gratitude has been linked to improved mental health. It reduces symptoms of depression and anxiety, promotes greater self-esteem and resilience, and enhances overall psychological well-being. By focusing on the positive aspects of our lives, gratitude helps us reframe negative experiences and find meaning in even the most challenging situations.

Furthermore, gratitude has a profound impact on our relationships. Expressing appreciation towards others strengthens our connections and fosters a sense of belonging. It deepens our empathy and compassion, making us more understanding and supportive individuals. As we cultivate gratitude, we become more attuned to the needs and feelings of those around us, leading to stronger and more fulfilling relationships.

In addition to its psychological and social benefits, gratitude also contributes to our physical health. Studies have shown that practicing gratitude leads to improved sleep, reduced stress levels, and a stronger immune system. By focusing on the positive aspects of our lives, we reduce the harmful effects of chronic stress and promote overall well-being.

In conclusion, the importance of being grateful cannot be overstated. By cultivating gratitude, we unlock the door to increased happiness and well-being. It not only improves our mental health and relationships but also has profound physical benefits. So, let us embark on this journey of gratitude together, and harness the power of thankfulness to create a life filled with joy, contentment, and success.

## Enhanced Relationships

In this subchapter, we delve into the powerful impact that gratitude has on enhancing relationships. Whether it's friendships, romantic partnerships, or even professional connections, gratitude has the ability to transform and strengthen these bonds in remarkable ways. By recognizing the importance of being grateful in our relationships, we can cultivate a deeper sense of connection, understanding, and harmony.

Gratitude is the key that unlocks the doors to our hearts and allows us to express appreciation for the people who bring joy, support, and love into our lives. It is through gratitude that we acknowledge the efforts and kindness of others, fostering a sense of mutual respect and admiration. When we express gratitude, we not only uplift the spirits of those around us but also create an environment that encourages reciprocity and a positive cycle of giving and receiving.

Furthermore, gratitude enables us to see beyond our own needs and desires, allowing us to empathize and understand the perspectives of others. It fosters compassion, patience, and forgiveness, which are essential attributes for building healthy and lasting relationships. By practicing gratitude, we become more attuned to the needs of our loved ones, and we develop the ability to provide the support and encouragement they require.

Moreover, gratitude acts as a powerful antidote to negativity and conflict within relationships. It helps us to let go of grudges, resentments, and negative emotions, enabling us to focus on the positive aspects of our connections instead. When we approach our relationships with a grateful mindset, we create a space for growth, understanding, and open communication, which are crucial for resolving conflicts and building trust.

In addition, gratitude strengthens our sense of belonging and deepens our emotional bonds. When we express gratitude, we reinforce the idea that we are valued and cherished, creating a sense of security and commitment within our relationships. This, in turn, fosters a deeper sense of intimacy and connection, allowing us to build stronger, more fulfilling relationships that stand the test of time.

In conclusion, the importance of being grateful in our relationships cannot be overstated. By embracing gratitude, we can transform our connections from surface-level interactions to profound and meaningful experiences. It is through gratitude that we cultivate empathy, compassion, and understanding, creating a solid foundation for lasting relationships filled with love, joy, and support. So, let us embark on this journey of enhanced relationships, where gratitude becomes the guiding force that transforms our lives and those around us.

**Physical Health Benefits**

Being grateful goes beyond just the emotional and psychological benefits; it also has a profound impact on our physical health. In this subchapter, we will explore the various ways in which gratitude can positively influence our well-being and overall physical health.

1. Boosts Immune System: Gratitude has been found to enhance the functioning of our immune system. Research suggests that individuals who practice gratitude regularly experience fewer symptoms of illness and have a stronger immune response. This can lead to a reduced risk of developing chronic diseases and a faster recovery from illness.

2. Reduces Stress: Chronic stress can have detrimental effects on our physical health. However, gratitude acts as a powerful antidote by reducing stress levels. When we focus on what we are thankful for, our bodies release feel-good hormones, such as oxytocin and dopamine, which counteract the harmful effects of stress hormones like cortisol.

3. Improves Sleep Quality: Many individuals struggle with sleep issues, which can negatively impact their overall health and well-being. Practicing gratitude before bed can help improve sleep quality. By shifting our focus to positive aspects of our lives, we calm our minds and promote relaxation, thus facilitating a restful night's sleep.

4. Enhances Heart Health: Gratitude has been linked to improved cardiovascular health. Expressing gratitude activates the parasympathetic nervous system, which promotes relaxation and lowers blood pressure. Additionally, gratitude encourages healthier lifestyle choices, such as regular exercise and a balanced diet, which further contribute to heart health.

5. Increases Energy Levels: When we embrace gratitude, we develop a positive outlook on life, which can lead to increased energy levels. The appreciation for the present moment and the good things in our lives can motivate us to engage in physical activities and adopt healthier habits. As a result, we experience higher levels of vitality and stamina.

6. Promotes Longevity: Studies have shown that grateful individuals tend to live longer and age more gracefully. The positive emotions associated with gratitude have a direct impact on our cellular health and can slow down the aging process. Gratitude also fosters a sense of purpose and meaning in life, which is essential for longevity.

In conclusion, the physical health benefits of gratitude are undeniable. By cultivating a grateful mindset, we can strengthen our immune system, reduce stress, improve sleep quality, enhance heart health, increase energy levels, and promote longevity. Embracing gratitude not only brings us joy and contentment but also ensures a healthier, happier life.

# Chapter 3: Gratitude for Personal Growth

## Developing Self-Awareness through Gratitude

In today's fast-paced and hectic world, it is easy to get caught up in the hustle and bustle of everyday life. We often find ourselves chasing after success, constantly striving for more without taking a moment to appreciate what we already have. However, the importance of being grateful cannot be overstated. Practicing gratitude not only improves our mental and emotional well-being, but it also helps us develop self-awareness and achieve greater success in life.

Gratitude is a powerful tool that allows us to shift our focus from what is lacking in our lives to what we already have. By cultivating a sense of gratitude, we become more aware of the abundance that surrounds us, even in the smallest of things. When we choose to acknowledge and appreciate the positive aspects of our lives, we start to develop a mindset of abundance rather than scarcity.

Through gratitude, we gain a deeper understanding of ourselves and our values. By taking time each day to reflect on the things we are grateful for, we become more aware of our priorities and what truly matters to us. This self-awareness helps us make better decisions aligned with our values and goals, leading to greater fulfillment and success.

Moreover, practicing gratitude allows us to cultivate a positive mindset. When we focus on gratitude, we train our minds to look for the good in every situation. This shift in perspective enables us to find opportunities and solutions where others may only see obstacles. A positive mindset not only enhances our problem-solving abilities but also inspires and motivates us to keep moving forward despite challenges.

In addition, gratitude strengthens our relationships with others. When we express gratitude and appreciation towards others, we create a positive and uplifting environment. People are naturally drawn to those who show genuine appreciation, and strong relationships are vital for personal and professional success. By nurturing our relationships through gratitude, we foster a supportive network that can help us achieve our goals.

In conclusion, developing self-awareness through gratitude is a powerful practice that can transform our lives. By focusing on the positive aspects of our lives, we gain a deeper understanding of ourselves, develop a positive mindset, and cultivate strong relationships. So, let us embrace the power of gratitude and harness its benefits to achieve greater success and fulfillment in our lives.

## Overcoming Challenges with Gratitude

In life, we all face challenges that can sometimes feel insurmountable. Whether it's a personal setback, a professional roadblock, or a global crisis, these challenges can leave us feeling overwhelmed and discouraged. However, there is a powerful tool that can help us navigate the toughest of times – gratitude.

Gratitude is the act of acknowledging and appreciating the positive aspects of our lives, even in the midst of difficulties. It is a mindset that allows us to shift our focus from what is going wrong to what is going right. When we cultivate gratitude, we open ourselves up to a world of possibilities and can overcome challenges with a renewed sense of strength and resilience.

One of the most important reasons to embrace gratitude is its ability to shift our perspective. When faced with a challenge, it is easy to get caught up in negative thinking and see only the obstacles in our path. However, by practicing gratitude, we can train our minds to look for the silver linings and opportunities for growth that often accompany challenges. This shift in perspective allows us to approach obstacles with a sense of optimism and determination, knowing that there is always something to be grateful for, even in the most difficult circumstances.

Furthermore, gratitude has a profound impact on our mental and emotional well-being. Research has shown that practicing gratitude can increase feelings of happiness, improve overall life satisfaction, and reduce symptoms of depression and anxiety. By actively cultivating a grateful mindset, we can build emotional resilience and better cope with the challenges that come our way. Gratitude acts as a protective shield, allowing us to navigate through tough times with grace and gratitude.

Moreover, gratitude fosters a sense of connection and empathy with others. When we practice gratitude, we acknowledge the support and kindness we receive from those around us. This recognition helps us build stronger relationships and fosters a sense of community. In times of challenge, having a supportive network can make all the difference. By expressing gratitude to others, we create a positive feedback loop, where acts of kindness and support are reciprocated, further enhancing our ability to overcome challenges.

In conclusion, the importance of being grateful cannot be overstated. In the face of challenges, cultivating gratitude can help us shift our perspective, improve our mental and emotional well-being, and strengthen our connections with others. By embracing gratitude, we can harness its power to overcome obstacles and find success in all areas of our lives. So, let us choose gratitude, even in the toughest of times, and experience the transformative effects it can have on our lives.

## Setting and Achieving Goals with Gratitude

In today's fast-paced world, it is easy to get caught up in the hustle and bustle of everyday life. We often find ourselves chasing after success, striving to achieve our goals, and constantly looking for ways to improve ourselves. But amidst this frenzy, we often forget to pause and reflect on the importance of being grateful.

Gratitude is a powerful emotion that can transform our lives and lead us to greater success and fulfillment. It is the practice of acknowledging and appreciating the good things in our lives, no matter how big or small. When we approach our goals with gratitude, we unlock a whole new level of motivation, focus, and positivity.

Setting goals is essential for personal and professional growth. However, many people make the mistake of solely focusing on the end result, neglecting the journey and the blessings along the way. By incorporating gratitude into goal setting, we shift our perspective from scarcity to abundance.

When we express gratitude for what we already have, we attract more of the same into our lives. This positive mindset allows us to see opportunities and possibilities that we may have otherwise missed. Gratitude also helps us stay motivated and committed to our goals, as we are constantly reminded of the blessings and progress we have made.

Achieving goals can be a challenging and sometimes frustrating process. However, by practicing gratitude, we can maintain a sense of perspective and optimism even in the face of setbacks. Instead of dwelling on what went wrong, we can focus on what we have learned and how far we have come.

Gratitude also enhances our relationships and connections with others. When we acknowledge and appreciate the support and encouragement we receive, we build stronger networks and attract like-minded individuals who can help us on our journey towards success.

To harness the power of gratitude in setting and achieving goals, it is essential to cultivate a daily gratitude practice. This can be as simple as keeping a gratitude journal, where we write down three things we are grateful for each day. By consistently acknowledging the good in our lives, we train our minds to focus on abundance and attract more of it.

In conclusion, incorporating gratitude into our goal-setting process is crucial for success and fulfillment. By practicing gratitude, we shift our perspective, attract more positive experiences, stay motivated, and build stronger connections. So let us embrace the power of thankfulness and harness the gratitude effect in our journey towards achieving our goals.

# Chapter 4: Gratitude in the Workplace

**Enhancing Employee Engagement through Gratitude**

In today's fast-paced and competitive world, businesses are constantly searching for ways to increase employee engagement and productivity. One powerful tool that often gets overlooked is gratitude. Gratitude not only benefits individuals on a personal level but also has a profound impact on the workplace environment. In this subchapter, we will explore the importance of being grateful and how it can enhance employee engagement.

Gratitude is a simple yet transformative concept. It involves acknowledging and appreciating the positive aspects of life, both big and small. When applied in the workplace, gratitude can create a culture of appreciation, foster stronger relationships, and ultimately improve employee satisfaction and performance.

Research has consistently shown that grateful individuals tend to be happier, healthier, and more resilient. When employees feel valued and appreciated, they are more likely to be motivated, committed, and loyal to their organization. Gratitude can help build trust and strengthen the bond between employees and their leaders, leading to increased collaboration and teamwork.

So how can organizations enhance employee engagement through gratitude? It starts with leadership. Managers and supervisors play a crucial role in creating a culture of gratitude. By expressing their appreciation for employees' efforts and contributions, leaders set the tone for the entire organization. This can be done through simple gestures such as saying "thank you" or recognizing outstanding performance publicly.

Another way to enhance employee engagement through gratitude is by implementing gratitude practices and rituals within the workplace. This can include regular team meetings where employees share what they are grateful for or creating a gratitude board where individuals can express their appreciation for their colleagues. These practices not only foster a sense of camaraderie but also remind employees of the positive aspects of their work environment.

Furthermore, organizations can incorporate gratitude into their employee recognition programs. Recognizing and rewarding employees for their hard work not only boosts morale but also reinforces a culture of appreciation. By acknowledging and celebrating achievements, organizations show their employees that their efforts are valued and recognized.

In conclusion, enhancing employee engagement through gratitude is a powerful strategy that can transform the workplace environment. By cultivating a culture of appreciation, organizations can foster stronger relationships, increase motivation, and ultimately improve overall employee satisfaction and performance. It is important for every individual, regardless of their position or industry, to recognize the importance of being grateful and harness the power of thankfulness for success.

## Fostering a Positive Work Culture with Gratitude

In today's fast-paced and highly competitive work environments, it is easy to get caught up in the daily grind and lose sight of the importance of gratitude. However, fostering a positive work culture with gratitude can have a profound impact on both individuals and organizations. In this subchapter, we will explore the significance of being grateful and how it can contribute to success in the workplace.

Gratitude is a powerful tool that can transform the way we approach our work and interactions with others. It allows us to recognize and appreciate the efforts of our colleagues, leading to increased morale and a sense of camaraderie. When individuals feel valued and appreciated, they are more likely to be motivated, engaged, and committed to their work. This, in turn, leads to higher productivity, improved teamwork, and ultimately, greater success for the organization as a whole.

Furthermore, gratitude has been shown to have numerous health benefits, both physically and mentally. Research has found that individuals who regularly practice gratitude experience lower levels of stress, increased happiness, and improved overall well-being. By fostering a work culture that encourages gratitude, organizations can create a positive and supportive environment that promotes employee satisfaction and reduces burnout.

One of the most effective ways to cultivate gratitude in the workplace is through recognition and appreciation programs. These programs can range from simple gestures such as saying thank you or giving praise publicly, to more formalized systems that involve rewards and incentives. By acknowledging the contributions of individuals and teams, organizations can reinforce positive behaviors and foster a sense of gratitude among employees.

Furthermore, leaders play a crucial role in creating a culture of gratitude. When leaders express gratitude and model appreciation for their team members, it sets a powerful example and encourages others to do the same. Leaders can also promote gratitude by creating opportunities for employees to share their appreciation for one another, such as team-building exercises or regular feedback sessions.

In conclusion, fostering a positive work culture with gratitude is essential for individual and organizational success. By embracing gratitude, organizations can create a supportive and engaging environment that promotes employee well-being and enhances overall performance. So, let us all remember the importance of being grateful and harness the power of thankfulness to create a fulfilling and successful work culture.

# Gratitude as a Tool for Leadership Development

In today's fast-paced and competitive world, leadership skills have become crucial for success in any field. Whether you are a business executive, a team leader, a teacher, or even a parent, being able to effectively lead and inspire others is essential. While there are many strategies and techniques for leadership development, one often overlooked tool is gratitude.

Gratitude is the practice of expressing appreciation and thankfulness for the people, experiences, and opportunities in our lives. It is a mindset that shifts our focus from what we lack to what we have, fostering a positive and optimistic outlook. When applied to leadership, gratitude has the power to transform both individuals and teams, helping them reach their full potential.

One of the greatest benefits of incorporating gratitude into leadership development is its ability to enhance relationships. Expressing gratitude towards team members, colleagues, or employees not only makes them feel valued and appreciated but also builds trust and loyalty. When people feel acknowledged and recognized for their efforts, they are more motivated to go above and beyond, leading to increased productivity and a positive work environment.

Moreover, gratitude fosters empathy and compassion, essential qualities for effective leaders. By recognizing and appreciating the strengths and contributions of others, leaders develop a deeper understanding of their team's needs and can provide the necessary support to help them thrive. This not only enhances individual performance but also strengthens the overall team dynamic, leading to improved collaboration and innovation.

In addition to relationship-building, gratitude also plays a significant role in personal growth and self-improvement. Leaders who practice gratitude are more self-aware and have a greater sense of clarity and purpose. They are able to reflect on their own strengths and weaknesses, leading to continuous learning and development. Furthermore, gratitude helps leaders stay grounded and resilient in the face of challenges, as they are able to recognize the lessons and opportunities for growth that arise from difficult situations.

In conclusion, gratitude is a powerful tool for leadership development that should not be underestimated. Its ability to enhance relationships, foster empathy, and promote personal growth makes it an essential practice for leaders in any field. By incorporating gratitude into our daily lives, we can create a positive and supportive environment that empowers individuals and teams to reach their full potential. So, let us embrace the importance of being grateful and harness the transformative power of thankfulness for success in our leadership journey.

# Chapter 5: Gratitude in Relationships

## Strengthening Romantic Relationships with Gratitude

In our modern and fast-paced world, it can be easy to take our romantic relationships for granted. We get caught up in our busy lives, and sometimes forget to express our gratitude for the love and support we receive from our partners. However, practicing gratitude can have a profound impact on the strength and longevity of our relationships.

Gratitude is the simple act of recognizing and appreciating the good things in our lives. When we apply this mindset to our romantic relationships, it allows us to focus on the positive aspects of our partnership and express our appreciation to our significant others.

One of the key benefits of practicing gratitude in our relationships is that it helps us to foster a sense of connection and intimacy. When we express our gratitude, we are essentially communicating to our partners that we value and cherish them. This can create a deep sense of emotional connection and strengthen the bond between two individuals.

Moreover, gratitude helps to cultivate a positive and supportive environment within a relationship. When we regularly show our appreciation for our partner's efforts, it encourages them to continue their loving gestures and behaviors. This positive reinforcement can lead to a cycle of gratitude, where both partners feel motivated to consistently show their love and appreciation for one another.

Gratitude also plays a crucial role in resolving conflicts and overcoming challenges in a relationship. When we approach disagreements with a grateful mindset, we are more likely to focus on finding a solution rather than dwelling on the negative aspects. By acknowledging and appreciating our partner's perspective, we can find common ground and work towards a resolution that satisfies both parties.

Furthermore, gratitude helps to create a sense of balance and perspective in our relationships. It reminds us to be mindful of the small gestures and acts of kindness that often go unnoticed. By consciously recognizing and expressing gratitude for these everyday moments, we can shift our focus from what may be lacking to what is present and meaningful in our relationship.

In conclusion, practicing gratitude is essential for strengthening romantic relationships. By expressing appreciation, fostering emotional connection, creating a positive environment, resolving conflicts, and maintaining perspective, we can cultivate a relationship built on love, respect, and mutual gratitude. So, let us embrace the power of gratitude and harness its potential to create fulfilling and long-lasting romantic partnerships.

## Nurturing Friendships through Gratitude

Friendships are an essential aspect of our lives, bringing joy, support, and a sense of belonging. As social beings, we thrive on human connections and the bond we share with our friends. However, in the hustle and bustle of everyday life, we often take these friendships for granted. It is crucial for us to recognize the importance of being grateful for the friendships we have and to actively nurture them through gratitude.

Gratitude is a powerful emotion that has the ability to transform our lives, including our relationships. When we express gratitude towards our friends, we not only strengthen the bond but also create a positive and nurturing environment for the friendship to flourish.

One of the key reasons why gratitude is essential in nurturing friendships is that it fosters a sense of appreciation. By expressing gratitude, we show our friends that we value and cherish their presence in our lives. This acknowledgment not only makes them feel valued but also encourages them to reciprocate, deepening the bond we share.

Moreover, gratitude acts as a catalyst for positivity. When we focus on the things we appreciate about our friends, it shifts our attention away from any grievances or conflicts. It allows us to see the good in them and promotes a harmonious and uplifting atmosphere within the friendship.

Practicing gratitude also cultivates empathy and understanding. When we take the time to recognize and be grateful for the qualities and actions of our friends, we develop a greater understanding of their perspective. This understanding enables us to communicate more effectively, resolve conflicts with compassion, and support them in times of need.

Additionally, gratitude acts as a reminder of the effort and time our friends invest in our friendship. It encourages us to reciprocate their kindness and support, fostering a sense of mutuality and balance in the relationship.

To nurture friendships through gratitude, it is important to make gratitude a daily practice. Take a moment each day to reflect on the qualities and actions of your friends that you are grateful for. Express your gratitude through heartfelt words, gestures, or small acts of kindness. Remember, gratitude is contagious, and by expressing it, you inspire others to do the same.

In conclusion, nurturing friendships through gratitude is a powerful way to strengthen the bonds we share with our friends. By recognizing the importance of being grateful for the friendships we have and actively expressing our gratitude, we create a positive and nurturing environment for the friendship to thrive. Let us cherish and cultivate the priceless gift of friendship through the transformative power of gratitude.

**Building Strong Family Bonds with Gratitude**

In our fast-paced and often chaotic lives, it can be easy to take our loved ones for granted. We get caught up in our daily routines, work, and personal struggles, forgetting to appreciate the people who mean the most to us. However, cultivating gratitude within our families can have a profound impact on our relationships and overall happiness. This subchapter aims to highlight the importance of being grateful for our loved ones and how it can help build strong family bonds.

Gratitude is more than just saying "thank you." It is a mindset, a way of viewing the world with appreciation and acknowledging the blessings we have. When we practice gratitude within our families, we create an environment of love, support, and understanding. It allows us to focus on the positive aspects of our relationships and encourages open communication.

Being grateful for our family members helps us to see their worth and value. It reminds us of the sacrifices they make for us, the love they shower upon us, and the joy they bring into our lives. By expressing our gratitude, whether through words, acts of kindness, or thoughtful gestures, we strengthen the bond between family members. It fosters a sense of belonging and a deep appreciation for one another.

Gratitude also teaches us empathy and compassion. When we are grateful for the presence of our loved ones, we become more aware of their needs and emotions. We become attuned to their struggles and joys, and we are more inclined to offer support and understanding. Gratitude allows us to connect on a deeper level, creating an atmosphere of trust and emotional intimacy.

Furthermore, gratitude helps us navigate through challenges and difficult times. When we face adversity, it is easy to become overwhelmed and lose sight of what truly matters. However, a grateful mindset allows us to find strength in our relationships and seek solace in the love and support of our family. It helps us appreciate the lessons we learn from hardships and find silver linings even in the darkest of times.

In conclusion, building strong family bonds with gratitude is essential for our overall well-being and happiness. It teaches us to cherish our loved ones, cultivates empathy and compassion, and provides a source of strength during challenging times. By practicing gratitude within our families, we create a nurturing and loving environment where everyone feels valued and appreciated. Let us embrace the power of gratitude and watch as it transforms our relationships and lives for the better.

# Chapter 6: Gratitude for Success and Achievement

## Harnessing Gratitude for Professional Success

In today's fast-paced and competitive world, it is easy to get caught up in the pursuit of professional success. We often find ourselves constantly striving for more, never truly satisfied with our achievements. However, amidst the chaos and ambition, we tend to overlook the importance of being grateful for the opportunities and successes that come our way.

Gratitude is a powerful tool that has the potential to transform our lives, especially when it comes to our professional endeavors. It allows us to shift our focus from what we lack to what we have, enabling us to appreciate the present moment and the progress we have made so far.

One of the key reasons why gratitude is essential for professional success is its ability to enhance our overall well-being. When we cultivate an attitude of gratitude, we experience higher levels of happiness, contentment, and fulfillment. This positive mindset not only improves our mental and emotional health but also boosts our productivity and performance in the workplace.

Moreover, expressing gratitude towards others plays a significant role in building strong professional relationships. People appreciate being acknowledged and recognized for their efforts, and showing gratitude can create a positive and supportive work environment. This, in turn, fosters collaboration, teamwork, and loyalty, ultimately leading to increased success and growth in our careers.

Gratitude also helps us to maintain a growth mindset, which is crucial for professional development. When we are grateful for our accomplishments, we are more likely to see setbacks and failures as opportunities for learning and growth. Rather than dwelling on our mistakes, we can approach challenges with resilience and a positive attitude, allowing us to bounce back stronger than ever.

In addition to these personal benefits, practicing gratitude also has a ripple effect on those around us. By expressing gratitude and appreciation towards our colleagues, mentors, and clients, we inspire and uplift them. This creates a cycle of positivity and success, as people are more inclined to support and collaborate with individuals who show genuine gratitude.

To harness the power of gratitude for professional success, it is important to incorporate gratitude practices into our daily lives. This can be as simple as keeping a gratitude journal, where we write down things we are grateful for each day. We can also make it a habit to express our gratitude to others through heartfelt thank-you notes or in-person appreciation.

In conclusion, embracing gratitude is a game-changer when it comes to professional success. By acknowledging and appreciating the opportunities and achievements we have, we can create a positive mindset, build strong relationships, and maintain a growth-oriented approach. So, let us harness the power of gratitude and watch as it transforms our professional lives, bringing us greater success, fulfillment, and happiness.

**Gratitude and Financial Abundance**

In today's fast-paced and materialistic world, it is easy to get caught up in the pursuit of financial success and material possessions. However, what many people fail to realize is that true financial abundance begins with gratitude. In this subchapter, we will explore the importance of being grateful for our financial circumstances and how it can lead to greater abundance and success.

Gratitude is a powerful force that can transform our lives in countless ways. When we are grateful for what we have, we shift our focus from what is lacking to what is already present. This shift in perspective allows us to attract more abundance into our lives. By appreciating the money and resources we currently have, we open ourselves up to receiving even more.

Being grateful for our financial circumstances does not mean settling for less or being complacent. Rather, it means recognizing and acknowledging the abundance that already exists in our lives. It is about finding contentment in the present moment while still striving for growth and improvement. When we cultivate an attitude of gratitude, we invite more opportunities for financial success and abundance to come our way.

Furthermore, gratitude helps us develop a positive mindset, which is essential for achieving financial goals. When we are grateful, we naturally align ourselves with abundance and prosperity, attracting more opportunities for financial growth. Our positive energy and outlook become magnets for success and wealth.

Practicing gratitude also helps us develop a healthy relationship with money. Instead of viewing money as a source of stress or anxiety, we can see it as a tool for creating a fulfilling and abundant life. By being grateful for the money we earn and the resources we have, we can make wiser financial decisions and use our resources in a way that aligns with our values and goals.

In conclusion, gratitude is a powerful catalyst for financial abundance. By appreciating what we already have and adopting a positive mindset, we create a fertile ground for success and prosperity. By cultivating gratitude in our financial lives, we can attract more opportunities, make wiser decisions, and ultimately experience greater financial abundance. So, let us embrace gratitude and harness its power for a life of success and fulfillment.

## Gratitude as a Catalyst for Personal Achievement

In today's fast-paced and demanding world, it is easy to get caught up in the pursuit of personal success and overlook the simple yet profound power of gratitude. It is said that being grateful is the key to unlocking a fulfilling and successful life. In this subchapter, we will explore the importance of being grateful and how it can serve as a catalyst for personal achievement.

Gratitude is a state of mind and a way of life that involves recognizing and appreciating the good things in our lives. It is an attitude that allows us to shift our focus from what we lack to what we have, from problems to opportunities, and from negativity to positivity. When we cultivate gratitude, we develop a mindset that is open to possibilities and more likely to attract success.

One of the reasons why gratitude is so powerful is because it changes our perception. Instead of dwelling on what is wrong or missing, we begin to see the abundance and blessings that surround us. This shift in perspective enables us to make better decisions, take more calculated risks, and seize opportunities that we might have otherwise missed. By embracing gratitude, we create a positive ripple effect in our lives that can lead to personal growth and achievement.

Moreover, gratitude has a profound impact on our mental and emotional well-being. It reduces stress, increases happiness, and improves overall mental health. When we are grateful, we are less likely to be consumed by negative emotions such as envy, greed, or resentment, which can hinder our progress. Instead, we become more optimistic, resilient, and motivated to take action towards our goals.

In the realm of personal achievement, gratitude serves as a powerful motivator. When we appreciate what we have accomplished so far, we are inspired to reach for even greater heights. Gratitude fuels our ambition and propels us to strive for excellence. It helps us maintain a positive mindset, even in the face of challenges and setbacks, which is essential for long-term success.

In conclusion, the importance of being grateful cannot be overstated. It is a mindset that has the potential to transform our lives and pave the way for personal achievement. By embracing gratitude, we can shift our focus, improve our mental and emotional well-being, and harness the power of thankfulness for success. So, let us cultivate an attitude of gratitude and watch as it becomes a catalyst for our personal growth and achievement.

# Chapter 7: Practicing Gratitude Daily

## Creating a Gratitude Journal

In this subchapter, we will explore the powerful practice of creating a gratitude journal and how it can transform your life. Whether you are a busy professional, a stay-at-home parent, or a student, this simple yet profound technique can be incorporated into your daily routine to enhance your overall well-being and success.

The importance of being grateful cannot be overstated. Gratitude is not just a fleeting feeling of appreciation; it is a mindset that positively impacts every aspect of our lives. When we cultivate gratitude, we shift our focus from what is lacking to what we already have. This shift in perspective allows us to experience more joy, contentment, and fulfillment in our lives.

A gratitude journal is a tool that helps us actively practice gratitude. It serves as a tangible reminder of the blessings and abundance that surround us. By taking a few moments each day to reflect on what we are grateful for, we train our minds to seek out and appreciate the positive aspects of our lives.

To create a gratitude journal, you will need a notebook or a dedicated space in your digital device. Begin by setting aside a few minutes each day, preferably in the morning or evening, to write down at least three things you are grateful for. These can be big or small, from simple pleasures like a warm cup of coffee to significant achievements or the love and support of your friends and family.

As you write, try to be specific and descriptive. Instead of just saying "I am grateful for my job," you could write, "I am grateful for my job because it allows me to use my skills and make a meaningful contribution to society." Adding details and emotions will deepen your connection to the things you appreciate.

Consistency is key when creating a gratitude journal. Make it a non-negotiable part of your routine, and over time, you will begin to notice the positive changes it brings to your life. You may find yourself more resilient in the face of challenges, more compassionate towards yourself and others, and more aware of the abundance that surrounds you.

In conclusion, creating a gratitude journal is a simple yet powerful practice that can enhance your overall well-being and success. By focusing on the positive aspects of your life and actively cultivating gratitude, you can experience more joy, contentment, and fulfillment. Start today, and watch as the gratitude effect transforms your life for the better.

## Expressing Gratitude to Others

In our fast-paced and often self-centered world, it is easy to overlook the simple act of expressing gratitude to others. Yet, the importance of being grateful cannot be emphasized enough. Gratitude not only has the power to transform our own lives, but it also has a profound impact on those around us. In this subchapter, we will explore the significance of expressing gratitude to others and how it can enhance our overall well-being and success.

First and foremost, expressing gratitude to others is a way of acknowledging the positive impact they have on our lives. Whether it is a friend, family member, colleague, or even a stranger, taking the time to appreciate and thank them for their kindness, support, or assistance can create a ripple effect of positivity. When we express gratitude, we not only uplift the spirits of others, but we also cultivate a sense of fulfillment and contentment within ourselves.

Moreover, expressing gratitude fosters stronger connections and relationships. When we express our thanks, we show that we value and appreciate the efforts and contributions of others. This, in turn, strengthens the bond between individuals, leading to deeper connections and a sense of belonging. By expressing gratitude, we create an environment of mutual respect and understanding, which can have a profound impact on our personal and professional lives.

Furthermore, expressing gratitude to others can have significant benefits for our own well-being. Studies have shown that practicing gratitude can improve mental health, increase resilience, and enhance overall life satisfaction. By focusing on the positive aspects of our lives and expressing gratitude for them, we shift our mindset from one of scarcity to abundance. This shift in perspective allows us to cultivate a more positive outlook, reduce stress, and increase our overall happiness.

In conclusion, the importance of expressing gratitude to others cannot be overstated. It not only benefits those we express gratitude towards but also enriches our own lives. By acknowledging the positive impact of others and taking the time to thank them, we foster stronger connections, cultivate a sense of fulfillment, and enhance our overall well-being. So, let us make a conscious effort to express our gratitude to those who have touched our lives, for in doing so, we unlock the power of thankfulness for success and happiness.

## Incorporating Gratitude Rituals into Your Life

Gratitude is a powerful force that can transform our lives in remarkable ways. When we make gratitude a daily practice, we invite more positivity, happiness, and success into our lives. In this subchapter, we will explore the significance of being grateful and learn how to incorporate gratitude rituals into our daily routines.

Gratitude is a mindset that allows us to appreciate and acknowledge the blessings and positive aspects of our lives. It shifts our focus from what we lack to what we have, cultivating a sense of abundance and fulfillment. Research has shown that practicing gratitude can improve our mental and physical health, boost our relationships, enhance our overall well-being, and even increase our chances of success.

To incorporate gratitude rituals into our lives, we must first develop a gratitude mindset. This involves consciously choosing to focus on the positive aspects of our lives and being mindful of the blessings we receive. One effective way to start is by keeping a gratitude journal. Each day, take a few moments to write down three things you are grateful for. This simple practice helps to rewire our brains to notice and appreciate the good things in our lives.

Another powerful gratitude ritual is expressing gratitude to others. Take time each day to express your appreciation to someone who has made a positive impact in your life. It can be a friend, family member, coworker, or even a stranger. A heartfelt thank you or a kind gesture can go a long way in strengthening relationships and spreading positivity.

Practicing gratitude can also be incorporated into our daily routines. For example, during your morning routine, take a few moments to reflect on three things you are grateful for. This sets a positive tone for the day ahead and helps you approach challenges with a grateful mindset. Additionally, before going to bed, reflect on the day and identify three moments or experiences you are grateful for. This practice helps to cultivate a sense of contentment and peace.

Incorporating gratitude rituals into our lives may require some effort and consistency, but the benefits are truly transformative. By embracing gratitude, we invite more joy, abundance, and success into our lives. Remember, gratitude is not just for special occasions or holidays; it is a lifelong practice that can bring happiness and fulfillment every day.

In conclusion, incorporating gratitude rituals into our lives is essential for our overall well-being and success. By adopting a gratitude mindset, keeping a gratitude journal, expressing appreciation to others, and integrating gratitude into our daily routines, we can harness the power of thankfulness and experience a profound shift in our lives. Let gratitude be your guiding force, and watch as your life transforms before your very eyes.

# Chapter 8: Overcoming Obstacles to Gratitude

## Dealing with Negativity and Resentment

Negativity and resentment are two powerful emotions that can hold us back from experiencing true happiness and success in life. In this subchapter, we will explore effective strategies for dealing with these negative emotions and harnessing the power of gratitude to overcome them.

Negativity is a common emotion that we all experience at some point in our lives. It can stem from a variety of sources, such as personal setbacks, criticism, or even comparison to others. However, dwelling on negativity only perpetuates a cycle of unhappiness and prevents us from moving forward. The first step in dealing with negativity is to acknowledge its presence and understand its impact on our lives. By doing so, we can begin to take control of our emotions and choose a more positive mindset.

One powerful tool for combating negativity is gratitude. Gratitude allows us to shift our focus from what is going wrong to what is going right in our lives. It is about finding the silver linings, even in the darkest of times. By practicing gratitude regularly, we can train our minds to see the positive aspects of our lives, no matter how small they may seem. This shift in perspective can have a profound impact on our overall well-being and success.

Resentment, on the other hand, is a deep-seated feeling of bitterness or anger towards someone or something. It often arises from a sense of injustice or unfairness. However, holding onto resentment only harms ourselves, as it drains our energy and hinders our ability to forge positive relationships. To overcome resentment, it is important to practice forgiveness and empathy. By understanding that everyone makes mistakes and harboring resentment only hurts ourselves, we can release the negative emotions and focus on personal growth and happiness.

In conclusion, dealing with negativity and resentment is crucial for our personal growth and success. By acknowledging their presence, practicing gratitude, and embracing forgiveness, we can break free from the shackles of negativity and resentment. The power of gratitude allows us to see the beauty in every situation, no matter how difficult, and empowers us to create a more fulfilling and successful life. So, let us embark on this journey of gratitude, leaving behind negativity and resentment, and embracing the power of thankfulness for a life of abundance and joy.

## Cultivating Gratitude during Difficult Times

In our journey through life, we all face challenges that can sometimes feel overwhelming. Whether it's the loss of a job, a health issue, or a personal setback, difficult times can test our resilience and push us to our limits. However, it is during these trying moments that cultivating gratitude becomes even more crucial.

Gratitude is not just a feeling; it is a mindset, a way of perceiving the world around us. When we practice gratitude, we shift our focus from what is lacking to what we already have. It is an acknowledgment of the blessings, big and small, that exist in our lives despite the hardships. Cultivating gratitude during difficult times can have profound effects on our mental, emotional, and even physical well-being.

One of the most important benefits of being grateful during challenging periods is that it helps us maintain a positive outlook. When we actively seek out the good in our lives, even in the midst of adversity, we reframe our experiences and find meaning in our struggles. This positive mindset not only helps us cope with difficulties but also allows us to grow and learn from them.

Furthermore, practicing gratitude during tough times helps us develop resilience. It reminds us of the times we have overcome obstacles in the past, reinforcing our belief in our own strength and capabilities. By focusing on what we are grateful for, we are better equipped to face and overcome the current challenges we are facing.

Gratitude also has a profound impact on our relationships, both personal and professional. Expressing gratitude towards others during difficult times strengthens our bonds and fosters a sense of community and support. It reminds us that we are not alone in our struggles and that we have people who care about us.

In the book "The Gratitude Effect: Harnessing the Power of Thankfulness for Success," we delve deeper into the importance of cultivating gratitude during difficult times. We explore practical strategies and exercises to help you develop a gratitude practice that is tailored to your unique circumstances. Through personal anecdotes and scientific research, we illustrate the transformative power of gratitude and how it can lead to success and happiness.

No matter who you are or what challenges you are facing, cultivating gratitude can make a significant difference in your life. It has the power to shift your perspective, strengthen your resilience, and deepen your relationships. Embrace the power of gratitude and discover how it can help you navigate through difficult times with grace and resilience.

## Overcoming Gratitude Blocks

Gratitude is a powerful force that has the ability to transform our lives for the better. It has been proven time and again that cultivating a grateful mindset can lead to increased happiness, improved relationships, and even enhanced physical and mental well-being. However, despite the numerous benefits of gratitude, many people find it challenging to fully embrace and practice gratitude in their daily lives. These challenges, known as gratitude blocks, can hinder our ability to experience the true power of thankfulness.

One common gratitude block is the belief that we don't have anything to be grateful for. In a world that often emphasizes scarcity and competition, it is easy to overlook the abundance that surrounds us. However, the truth is that even in our darkest moments, there is always something to be grateful for. It may be as simple as a warm cup of coffee in the morning or a kind word from a friend. By shifting our focus from what we lack to what we have, we can start to break through this gratitude block and open ourselves up to the countless blessings that exist in our lives.

Another gratitude block that many people face is the tendency to take things for granted. We often become so accustomed to the blessings in our lives that we fail to appreciate them fully. This can lead to a sense of entitlement and a lack of gratitude. Overcoming this gratitude block requires us to cultivate a sense of mindfulness and presence. By consciously acknowledging and appreciating the small and big things in our lives, we can prevent ourselves from taking them for granted and instead nurture a deep sense of gratitude.

Fear and negativity are also common gratitude blocks that can hinder our ability to be grateful. When we are consumed by fear or negativity, it becomes difficult to see the positive aspects of our lives. Overcoming these blocks requires a conscious effort to reframe our thoughts and focus on the good. This may involve practicing affirmations, surrounding ourselves with positive influences, or seeking professional help if needed. By addressing and overcoming our fears and negativity, we can create space for gratitude to flourish.

In conclusion, overcoming gratitude blocks is crucial for harnessing the power of thankfulness for success. By recognizing and addressing these blocks, we can shift our mindset and open ourselves up to a world of abundance and positivity. Whether it's the belief that we lack things to be grateful for, taking blessings for granted, or being consumed by fear and negativity, every one of us can benefit from overcoming these gratitude blocks. The journey towards a grateful life begins with acknowledging the blocks and taking conscious steps to overcome them. Embracing gratitude will not only enhance our own well-being but also positively impact the lives of those around us.

# Chapter 9: Spreading the Gratitude Effect

## Teaching Gratitude to Children

In today's fast-paced and materialistic world, it is becoming increasingly important to instill the virtue of gratitude in children. Gratitude is the act of expressing appreciation for the positive aspects of one's life, and it holds immense power in shaping a person's mindset and overall well-being. As parents, educators, and caregivers, it is our responsibility to teach children the importance of being grateful.

The significance of being grateful cannot be emphasized enough. When children learn to appreciate the things they have, they develop a positive outlook on life. Gratitude helps them focus on the positives rather than dwelling on what they lack, which in turn cultivates resilience and happiness. It has been scientifically proven that grateful individuals experience lower levels of stress, anxiety, and depression. By teaching gratitude to children, we equip them with valuable tools to navigate life's challenges with grace and optimism.

Children learn best through observation and practice. Therefore, it is crucial for adults to model gratitude in their own lives. Expressing gratitude for everyday things like a beautiful sunset, a kind gesture, or a delicious meal teaches children the art of finding joy in the simple pleasures. Encouraging them to keep a gratitude journal, where they can write down the things they are thankful for each day, helps reinforce this habit and cultivates a sense of mindfulness.

Furthermore, incorporating gratitude rituals into daily routines can have a profound impact on children's well-being. This can be as simple as sharing one thing they are grateful for during family meals or bedtime discussions. By doing so, children learn to reflect on the positive aspects of their lives and develop a sense of appreciation for the people and experiences that bring them joy.

It is also essential to teach children empathy and compassion, as these qualities go hand in hand with gratitude. By encouraging acts of kindness and teaching them to appreciate the efforts of others, we foster a sense of interconnectedness and gratitude for the relationships in their lives.

In conclusion, teaching gratitude to children is a fundamental aspect of their emotional and mental development. By emphasizing the importance of being grateful, we equip them with the tools to lead fulfilling and meaningful lives. Through modeling gratitude, incorporating gratitude rituals, and fostering empathy, we can empower the next generation to embrace gratitude as a way of life, ultimately reaping the countless benefits it offers.

## Sharing Gratitude in Your Community

Gratitude is a powerful force that has the ability to transform lives and communities. In a world that often focuses on negativity and scarcity, the importance of being grateful cannot be overstated. When we express gratitude, we not only uplift ourselves but also inspire those around us to embrace a more positive outlook on life. This subchapter explores the significance of sharing gratitude in your community and the profound impact it can have on individuals and society as a whole.

One of the first steps in sharing gratitude in your community is to cultivate a personal practice of thankfulness. Take a moment each day to reflect on the things you are grateful for, whether it be your health, supportive relationships, or the simple pleasures in life. By nurturing this practice, you will develop a genuine sense of appreciation that will naturally overflow into your interactions with others.

Sharing gratitude can take many forms. It can be as simple as expressing a heartfelt "thank you" to the people who make a difference in your life, such as family, friends, or colleagues. Acts of kindness and appreciation go a long way in building strong and supportive communities. A small gesture of gratitude can brighten someone's day and create a ripple effect of positivity.

Another way to share gratitude in your community is by actively participating in community service or volunteer work. By giving back to those in need, you not only express gratitude for the blessings in your own life but also inspire others to do the same. Engaging in acts of service not only benefits the community but also deepens your own sense of gratitude and fulfillment.

Furthermore, creating a culture of gratitude in your community can have far-reaching effects. Encourage others to share their own stories of gratitude and inspire them to adopt a more grateful mindset. Organize gratitude circles or events where individuals can come together to express their appreciation and share their experiences. By fostering an environment of gratitude, you create a supportive network that amplifies the positive impact of thankfulness.

In conclusion, sharing gratitude in your community is a powerful way to promote positivity, foster strong relationships, and create a sense of belonging. By actively cultivating a personal practice of thankfulness, expressing gratitude to others, engaging in acts of service, and creating a culture of gratitude, you can harness the power of thankfulness for success in your community. Embrace the importance of being grateful and watch as it transforms not only your own life but also the lives of those around you.

## Creating a Ripple Effect of Gratitude

In our fast-paced and often chaotic world, it's easy to get caught up in the hustle and bustle of our daily lives. We often forget to pause and appreciate the simple things, the people who have helped us along the way, and the blessings we have been given. However, cultivating a sense of gratitude is not only important for our personal well-being but also has the power to positively impact every aspect of our lives.

The importance of being grateful cannot be overstated. Taking the time to acknowledge and appreciate the good things in our lives can significantly improve our mental and emotional well-being. Research has shown that practicing gratitude can reduce stress levels, increase happiness, and even improve physical health. When we are grateful, we shift our focus from what is lacking to what we already have, and this shift in perspective allows us to experience greater joy and contentment.

But the impact of gratitude goes far beyond our personal well-being. When we express gratitude towards others, we create a ripple effect that spreads positivity and kindness. Our gestures of appreciation have the power to touch the lives of those around us, inspiring them to also be grateful and pass on the kindness. Imagine a world where everyone took a moment each day to express gratitude to someone else – the impact would be tremendous.

Being grateful also enhances our relationships. When we express gratitude towards our loved ones, colleagues, or even strangers, we strengthen the bonds between us. Appreciation fosters a sense of connection and encourages others to continue their positive actions. It creates a harmonious and supportive environment where everyone feels valued and motivated to contribute their best.

So how do we create a ripple effect of gratitude? It starts with a conscious decision to practice gratitude daily. We can begin by keeping a gratitude journal, where we write down three things we are thankful for each day. This simple act of reflection helps us focus on the positive aspects of our lives and trains our minds to seek out gratitude. We can also make it a habit to express appreciation to those around us – a heartfelt thank you or a kind note can make someone's day and inspire them to pay it forward.

In conclusion, the importance of being grateful cannot be emphasized enough. Cultivating a sense of gratitude not only benefits our personal well-being but also has a profound impact on our relationships and the world around us. By creating a ripple effect of gratitude, we can spread positivity, kindness, and joy, making our lives and the lives of others richer and more fulfilling. Let us embrace the power of gratitude and harness it for our own success and the success of those around us.

# Chapter 10: The Gratitude Journey Continues

## Reinforcing Gratitude Habits

In today's fast-paced and highly competitive world, it's easy to get caught up in the never-ending cycle of striving for success and accomplishment. However, amidst the chaos, we often forget the importance of being grateful for the blessings that surround us. Cultivating an attitude of gratitude can have a profound impact on our lives, leading to increased happiness, improved relationships, and even greater success. This subchapter explores the significance of reinforcing gratitude habits and how they can positively shape our lives.

Gratitude is not just a fleeting feeling or a momentary expression of thanks; it is a powerful mindset that can transform our entire outlook on life. By actively practicing gratitude, we train our minds to focus on the positive aspects of our lives, rather than dwelling on the negatives. This shift in perspective allows us to appreciate what we have and find contentment in the present moment, leading to a more fulfilling and meaningful existence.

One effective way to reinforce gratitude habits is by incorporating a gratitude journal into our daily routine. Taking a few minutes each day to reflect on the things we are grateful for can significantly impact our mental and emotional well-being. Whether it is a loving family, good health, supportive friends, or even the simple pleasure of a beautiful sunset, acknowledging and appreciating these blessings helps us cultivate a deep sense of gratitude.

Another powerful habit to reinforce gratitude is to practice random acts of kindness. By extending a helping hand to others without expecting anything in return, we not only make a positive impact on their lives but also experience a sense of gratitude for the opportunity to make a difference. From volunteering at a local charity to simply offering a kind word or gesture to someone in need, these acts of kindness not only reinforce our gratitude but also create a ripple effect of positivity in the world around us.

Additionally, surrounding ourselves with like-minded individuals who also value gratitude can further reinforce this habit. By seeking out communities, support groups, or even online forums focused on gratitude, we can exchange stories, experiences, and tips for nurturing a grateful mindset. This sense of camaraderie and shared values can provide encouragement and accountability as we continue to reinforce our gratitude habits.

In conclusion, reinforcing gratitude habits is essential for leading a fulfilling and successful life. By actively practicing gratitude, incorporating a gratitude journal, performing random acts of kindness, and surrounding ourselves with a supportive community, we can cultivate an attitude of gratitude that permeates every aspect of our lives. Through this powerful shift in mindset, we can harness the transformative power of thankfulness and enjoy a more joyful and prosperous existence. So, let us all embrace gratitude and experience the profound effect it has on our lives.

## Embracing a Lifetime of Thankfulness

In this subchapter, we delve into the profound concept of embracing a lifetime of thankfulness. Gratitude is not a fleeting emotion; it is a way of life that can transform every aspect of our being. It is a mindset that, when cultivated, can lead to remarkable success and fulfillment. This subchapter aims to highlight the importance of being grateful and how it can positively impact everyone, regardless of their background or circumstances.

Gratitude is a powerful force that has the ability to shift our focus from what is lacking in our lives to what we already have. It allows us to appreciate the simple joys and blessings that surround us each day. By embracing a lifetime of thankfulness, we open ourselves up to the endless possibilities that gratitude brings forth.

Being grateful has numerous benefits, both on a personal and professional level. It enhances our overall well-being, improves our relationships, and boosts our mental and physical health. When we acknowledge and appreciate the goodness in our lives, we attract more positive experiences and opportunities. Gratitude becomes a catalyst for success, propelling us forward on our journey towards achieving our goals and dreams.

This subchapter will explore practical strategies and exercises to cultivate a mindset of gratitude. It will provide guidance on how to develop a gratitude journal, practice daily affirmations, and express appreciation to others. Additionally, it will emphasize the significance of gratitude in overcoming challenges and adversity. By embracing a lifetime of thankfulness, we can navigate through life's ups and downs with resilience and grace.

Moreover, this subchapter will debunk the misconception that gratitude is solely reserved for times of abundance and prosperity. It will shed light on the importance of being grateful even during difficult times, as it fosters resilience and helps us find silver linings amidst adversity. Gratitude is a powerful tool that enables us to find meaning and purpose in every situation, no matter how challenging it may seem.

In conclusion, embracing a lifetime of thankfulness is a transformative journey that can bring about profound change in our lives. By cultivating a mindset of gratitude, we unlock the power to attract success, enhance our well-being, and strengthen our relationships. This subchapter serves as a guide for everyone, regardless of their background, to harness the power of thankfulness and embark on a path towards a more fulfilling and successful life.

# Gratitude as a Transformational Tool for Success

In a world that often seems consumed by negativity and dissatisfaction, it is easy to overlook the importance of gratitude. However, cultivating a sense of thankfulness can be a powerful transformational tool that can lead to unparalleled success and fulfillment in all aspects of life. This subchapter delves into the significance of embracing gratitude and how it can positively impact our lives.

Gratitude is more than just saying "thank you" or expressing appreciation for what we have. It is a mindset, a way of perceiving the world around us. When we adopt an attitude of gratitude, we shift our focus from what is lacking to what is present in our lives. This shift in perspective enhances our ability to recognize opportunities, forge meaningful connections, and find joy in even the smallest of things.

One of the key benefits of gratitude is its ability to enhance our overall well-being. Research has consistently shown that individuals who practice gratitude experience higher levels of happiness, improved mental health, and reduced stress. By acknowledging and appreciating the good in our lives, we become more resilient in the face of challenges and are better equipped to navigate through setbacks.

Furthermore, gratitude has a profound impact on our relationships. When we express gratitude towards others, we strengthen our connections and foster a sense of belonging. Gratitude not only deepens existing relationships, but it also attracts new ones. People are naturally drawn to those who radiate positivity and appreciation, making gratitude an invaluable tool for building and nurturing a strong support network.

In the pursuit of success, gratitude acts as a catalyst for growth and achievement. By acknowledging the contributions of others, we create an atmosphere of collaboration and teamwork that propels us towards our goals. Gratitude also cultivates a mindset of abundance, enabling us to see opportunities where others see obstacles. This mindset shift opens up new possibilities and allows us to tap into our full potential.

Moreover, gratitude fuels motivation and perseverance. When we realize how much we have been blessed with, we are inclined to make the most of our opportunities and strive for excellence. Gratitude provides the drive necessary to overcome obstacles, embrace challenges, and persist in the face of adversity.

In conclusion, gratitude is a transformational tool that can bring about profound changes in our lives. By embracing gratitude, we can experience enhanced well-being, build stronger relationships, and unlock our full potential for success. So, let us take a moment each day to reflect on the blessings in our lives and express our gratitude. The power of thankfulness is immense, and it has the potential to positively impact every aspect of our existence.

www.ingramcontent.com/pod-product-compliance
Lightning Source LLC
Chambersburg PA
CBHW070314160726
47999CB00003B/1021